Selena Gómez

Actress and Singer / Actriz y cantante

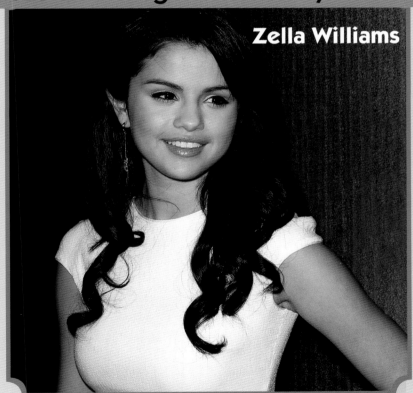

Zella Williams

PowerKiDS press™ & **Editorial Buenas Letras**™
New York

Published in 2011 by The Rosen Publishing Group, Inc.
29 East 21st Street, New York, NY 10010

First Edition

Editor: Joanne Randolph
Book Design: Kate Laczynski
Photo Researcher: Jessica Gerweck
Spanish Translation: Eduardo Alamán

Photo Credits: Cover, pp. 1, 13 (top) Jason LaVeris/FilmMagic/Getty Images; pp. 4, 5 Theo Wargo/Wireimage/Getty Images; pp. 6, 10 Jon Kopaloff/FilmMagic/Getty Images; p. 7 Michael Tran/FilmMagic/Getty Images; pp. 9, 20 Mathew Imaging/Wireimage/Getty Images; p. 11 Mark Perlstein/Time & Life Pictures/Getty Images; pp. 12, 13 (bottom) Frederick M. Brown/Getty Images; p. 14 Todd Williamson/Wireimage/Getty Images; p. 15 George Pimentel/Wireimage/Getty Images; p. 16 Ray Tamarra/Getty Images; p. 17 Kevin Winter/Getty Images; p. 18 Mark Sullivan/Wireimage/Getty Images; p. 19 Brian Ach/Wireimage/Getty Images; p. 21 (top) Robert Benson/Getty Images; p. 21 (bottom) John Shearer/Wireimage/Getty Images; p. 22 Jesse Grant/Wireimage/Getty Images.

Library of Congress Cataloging-in-Publication Data
Williams, Zella.
 Selena Gomez : actress and singer = actriz y cantante / Zella Williams. — 1st [bilingual] ed.
    p. cm. — (Hispanic headliners = Hispanos en las noticias)
 Includes webliography and index.
 ISBN 978-1-4488-4895-9 (paperback Selena Gomez/America Ferrera)
 1. Gomez, Selena, 1992—Juvenile literature. 2. Actors—United States–Biography—Juvenile literature.
 3. Singers—United States—Biography—Juvenile literature. I. Title.
 PN2287.G585W5518 2010
 791.4302'8092—dc22
 [B]
                                    2010010383
Manufactured in China

CPSIA Compliance Information: Batch #WS10PK: For Further Information contact Rosen Publishing, New York, New York at 1-800-237-9932

CONTENTS

CONTENIDO

Have you ever heard of Selena Gomez? If you have seen her work, then maybe you are a fan. She has played lots of parts on TV and in movies. She is best known for her work on *Wizards of Waverly Place*. She also sings in a band. She is just getting started, though. You may have heard some of her songs on the radio. If you have not heard of her yet, then you will!

Selena Gomez knew she wanted to become an actress at a young age.

Desde pequeña, Selena Gómez sabía que quería ser actriz.

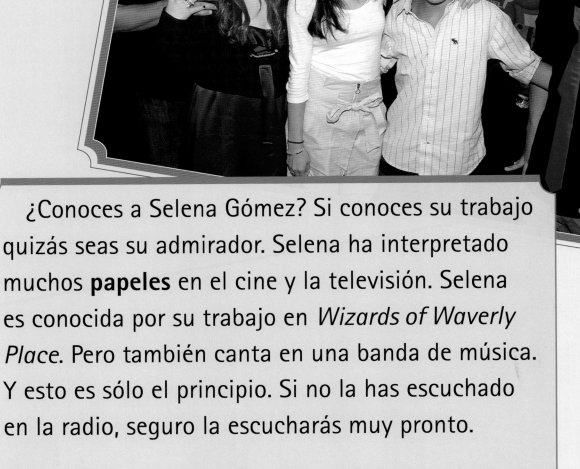

Gomez is shown here with some of the other actors from *Wizards of Waverly Place*.

Aquí vemos a Gómez con algunos de los actores de *Wizards of Waverly Place*.

¿Conoces a Selena Gómez? Si conoces su trabajo quizás seas su admirador. Selena ha interpretado muchos **papeles** en el cine y la televisión. Selena es conocida por su trabajo en *Wizards of Waverly Place*. Pero también canta en una banda de música. Y esto es sólo el principio. Si no la has escuchado en la radio, seguro la escucharás muy pronto.

Selena Gomez was born on July 22, 1992, to Mandy Cornett and Ricardo Gomez. She was born in New York City. Soon her family moved to Grand Prairie, Texas, though. This is where Mandy Cornett's family lived. Mandy was only 16 when she had Selena. They did not have a lot of money during that time.

Selena's father, Ricardo Gomez, has family in Guadalajara, Jalisco, Mexico.

El papá de Selena, Ricardo Gómez, tiene familia en Guadalajara, Jalisco, México.

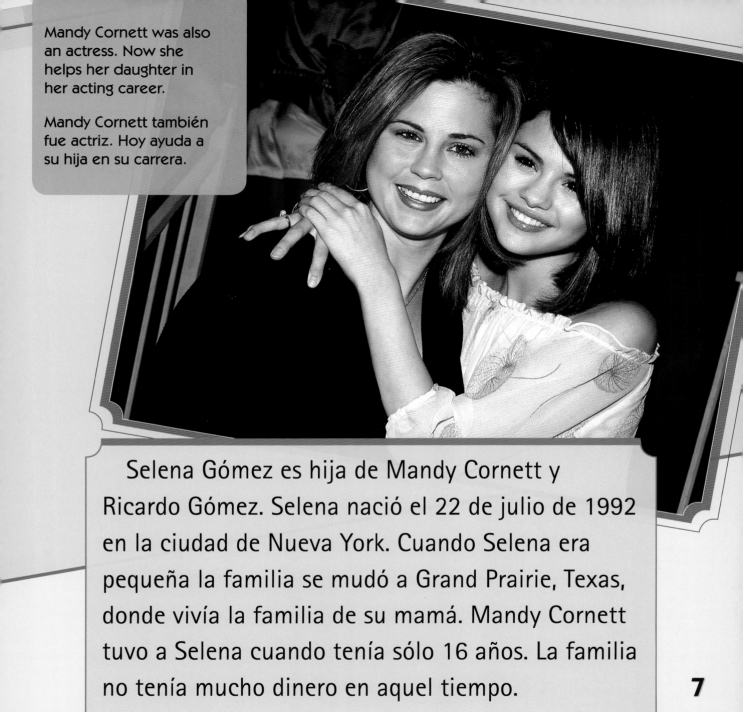

Mandy Cornett was also an actress. Now she helps her daughter in her acting career.

Mandy Cornett también fue actriz. Hoy ayuda a su hija en su carrera.

Selena Gómez es hija de Mandy Cornett y Ricardo Gómez. Selena nació el 22 de julio de 1992 en la ciudad de Nueva York. Cuando Selena era pequeña la familia se mudó a Grand Prairie, Texas, donde vivía la familia de su mamá. Mandy Cornett tuvo a Selena cuando tenía sólo 16 años. La familia no tenía mucho dinero en aquel tiempo.

7

Selena Gomez's parents **divorced** in 1997, when Selena was five. Her mother was an actress in the theater. Selena often went with her mother to **rehearsals**. It was during this time that Selena decided she would like to become an actress, too. Her wish came true sooner than she might have thought it would.

Gomez's mother married Brian Teefy, who became Gomez's stepfather, in 2006.

La mamá de Gómez se casó con Brian Teefy, que se convirtió en su padrastro, en 2006.

Los papás de Selena se **divorciaron** en 1997, cuando tenía cinco años. Su mamá era actriz de teatro. Con frecuencia, Selena iba con ella a sus **ensayos**. Fue durante estos días que Selena decidió que ella también quería ser actriz. Su deseo se hizo realidad antes de lo que ella esperaba.

When Selena turned seven, she got a **role** as Gianna on *Barney & Friends*. She appeared in this role many times. The shows did not air until she was in fifth grade, though. Over the next few years, she got more small parts. One of these parts was in *SpyKids 3-D: Game Over*, in 2003.

Once Selena got the part as Gianna, she started getting more parts.

Después de obtener el papel de Gianna, Selena comenzó a obtener más papeles.

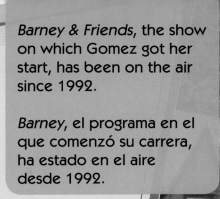

Barney & Friends, the show on which Gomez got her start, has been on the air since 1992.

Barney, el programa en el que comenzó su carrera, ha estado en el aire desde 1992.

A los siete años, Selena obtuvo el papel de Gianna en *Barney*. Selena apareció en este programa muchas veces. Estos programas no se transmitieron hasta que Selena estuvo en quinto grado. En los siguientes años, Selena obtuvo muchos otros papeles. Uno de estos fue en 2003, en *SpyKids 3-D: Game Over*.

11

In 2004, Selena Gomez started getting small parts on shows on the Disney Channel. She was in *The Suite Life of Zach & Cody* and *Hannah Montana*. Then, in 2007, Selena landed her own show. She took a part as Alex Russo on *Wizards of Waverly Place.* In this show, Alex and her brothers are learning to use their magical powers.

In 2009, *Wizards of Waverly Place* won an Emmy Award.

Wizards of Waverly Place ganó el premio Emmy en 2009.

One of Gomez's costars on *Wizards of Waverly Place* is Jake T. Austin, shown with her here.

Aquí vemos a Gómez con su compañero Jake T. Austin de *Wizards of Waverly Place*.

Selena comenzó a obtener pequeñas partes en el canal de Disney en 2004. Selena estuvo en *The Suite Life of Zach & Cody* y en *Hannah Montana*. En 2007, Selena consiguió su propio programa, en el papel de Alex Russo en *Wizards of Waverly Place*. En este programa, Alex y sus hermanos tienen poderes mágicos.

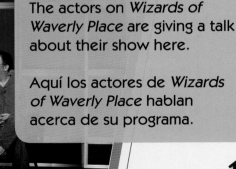

The actors on *Wizards of Waverly Place* are giving a talk about their show here.

Aquí los actores de *Wizards of Waverly Place* hablan acerca de su programa.

In 2008, Selena Gomez took a part in *Another Cinderella Story*. She also had movie roles in *Princess Protection Program* and *Wizards of Waverly Place: The Movie*. In 2009, she got a part in *Ramona and Beezus*, based on a book by Beverly Cleary. She has done some voice acting for movies, too, including *Horton Hears a Who!*

Gomez and her friend Taylor Swift during a showing of *Another Cinderella Story*.

Gómez y su amiga Taylor Swift durante una presentación de *Another Cinderella Story*.

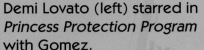

Demi Lovato (left) starred in *Princess Protection Program* with Gomez.

Demi Lovato (izquierda) actuó con Gómez en *Princess Protection Program.*

En 2008, Selena actuó en *Another Cinderella Story*. Además tuvo papeles en *Princess Protection Program* y la película de *Wizards of Waverly Place*. En 2009, obtuvo un papel en *Ramona and Beezus*, que se basó en un libro de Beverly Cleary. ¡Además, Selena ha prestado su voz para el cine, como en la película *Horton Hears a Who!*

15

Selena Gomez does more than act. She also sings and dances. In 2008, she started a band called Selena Gomez & the Scene. The band's first album came out in September 2009. It is called *Kiss & Tell*. It sold 66,000 copies in the first week! Gomez has also recorded songs for some movie sound tracks. Some of these were for movies she had a part in but some were not.

Gomez sang a song from her first album on a TV talk show called *Good Morning America*.

Gómez canta una canción de su primer álbum en el programa de televisión *Good Morning America*.

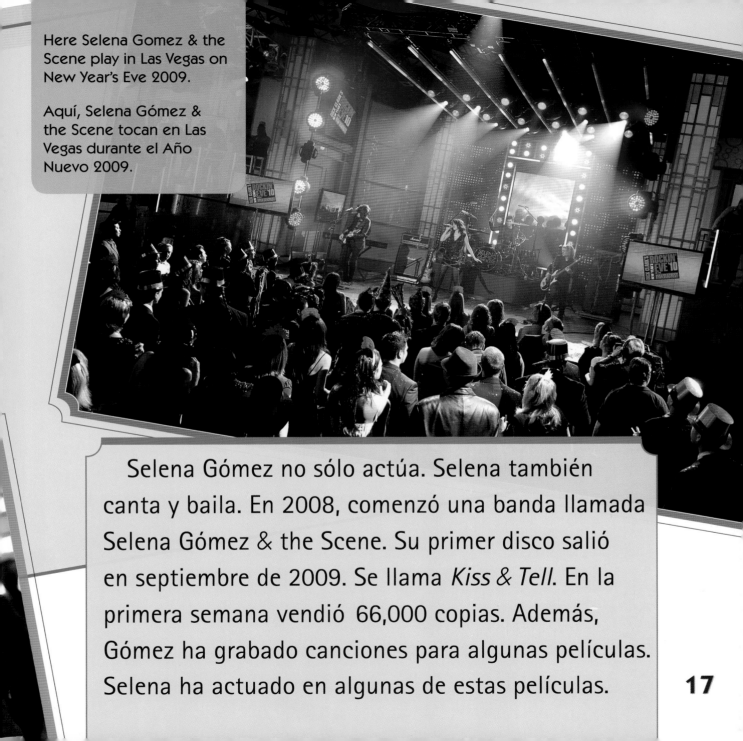

Here Selena Gomez & the Scene play in Las Vegas on New Year's Eve 2009.

Aquí, Selena Gómez & the Scene tocan en Las Vegas durante el Año Nuevo 2009.

Selena Gómez no sólo actúa. Selena también canta y baila. En 2008, comenzó una banda llamada Selena Gómez & the Scene. Su primer disco salió en septiembre de 2009. Se llama *Kiss & Tell*. En la primera semana vendió 66,000 copias. Además, Gómez ha grabado canciones para algunas películas. Selena ha actuado en algunas de estas películas.

17

Selena Gomez also does a lot of **charity** work. She helped in the UR Votes Count **campaign** in 2008. This campaign tried to get young people to learn more about presidential candidates. It also encouraged them to vote. She was named one of UNICEF's goodwill **ambassadors** in 2009.

A young girl gave Gomez this card at a UR Votes Count event.

Una chica le dió a Gómez esta tarjeta en un evento de UR Votes Count.

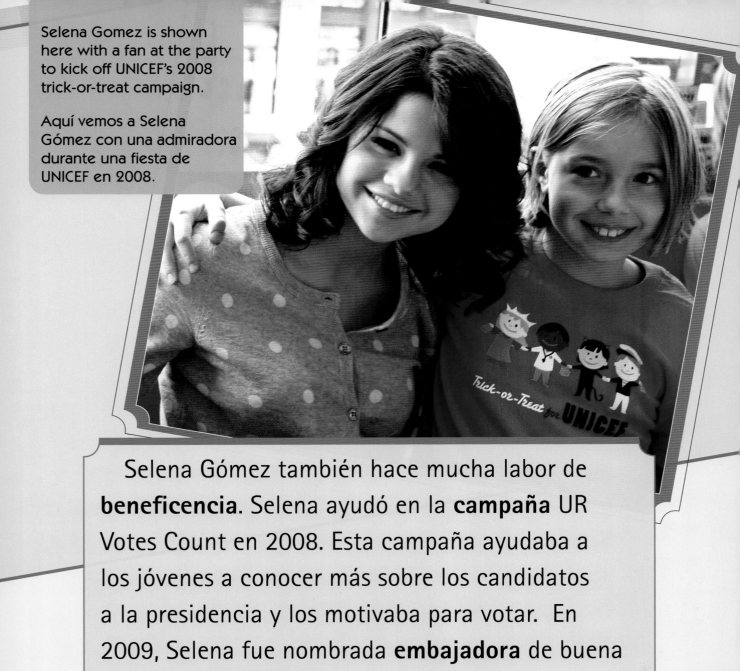

Selena Gomez is shown here with a fan at the party to kick off UNICEF's 2008 trick-or-treat campaign.

Aquí vemos a Selena Gómez con una admiradora durante una fiesta de UNICEF en 2008.

Selena Gómez también hace mucha labor de **beneficencia**. Selena ayudó en la **campaña** UR Votes Count en 2008. Esta campaña ayudaba a los jóvenes a conocer más sobre los candidatos a la presidencia y los motivaba para votar. En 2009, Selena fue nombrada **embajadora** de buena voluntad de UNICEF.

19

Selena Gomez has been **nominated** for and won many awards for her work. She won a Kid's Choice Award in 2009 for *Wizards of Waverly Place*. She won some Teen Choice Awards that year, too. She has also been nominated for Alma and Imagen awards for her work as a Latina artist.

Here the actors from *Wizards of Waverly Place* show off their Emmy Awards.

Aquí vemos a los actores de *Wizards of Waverly Place* mostrando sus premios Emmy.

Selena Gomez is shown here thanking people for her 2009 Alma Award.

Selena Gómez agradece por su premio Alma en 2009.

Selena Gómez ha ganado muchos premios. Selena ganó el Kid's Choice Award en 2009 por *Wizards of Waverly Place*. Ese año también ganó algunos Teen Choice Awards. Además ha sido **nominada** para los premios Alma e Imagen por su trabajo como artista latina.

Here Gomez receives her 2009 Teen Choice Award.

Aquí Gómez recibe su Teen Choice Award en 2009.

21

We are sure to see a lot more from Selena Gomez. She already has her own production company, called July Moon Productions. She also has a clothing line, called Dream Out Loud by Selena Gomez. What else will she do? The sky is the limit for this young actress and singer!

Seguramente veremos mucho más de Selena Gómez. Selena ya tiene su propia casa productora, llamada July Moon Productions. También tiene una marca de ropa llamada Dream Out Loud por Selena Gómez. ¿Qué más podría hacer Selena? ¡Para esta joven estrella el cielo es el límite!

GLOSSARY

ambassadors (am-BA-suh-durz) People who are voices for countries or groups and who visit other countries or groups to share a message.

campaign (kam-PAYN) A plan to get a certain result, such as to win an election.

charity (CHER-uh-tee) A generous act.

divorced (dih-VORST) Ended a marriage.

nominated (NO-muh-nayt-ed) Picked to do a certain job.

rehearsals (rih-HER-sulz) Practices for something, such as a play.

role (ROHL) A part played by a person or thing.

GLOSARIO

beneficencia Un acto de generosidad.

campaña (la) Un plan para obtener un resultado.

divorcio (el) Terminar un matrimonio.

embajadora (la) Una persona que representa a un grupo o país para visitar otros países para transmitir un mensaje.

ensayos (los) Practicar para algo, como una obra de teatro.

nominada Ser elegida para una posición u honor.

papel (el) La parte representada por una persona.

INDEX

ÍNDICE

WEB SITES / PÁGINAS DE INTERNET

Due to the changing nature of Internet links, PowerKids Press and Editorial Buenas Letras have developed an online list of Web sites related to the subject of this book. This site is updated regularly. Please use this link to access the list: www.powerkidslinks.com/hh/gomez/

Hispanic Headliners ◆ Hispanos en las noticias

América Ferrera

Award-Winning Actress / Estrella de la pantalla

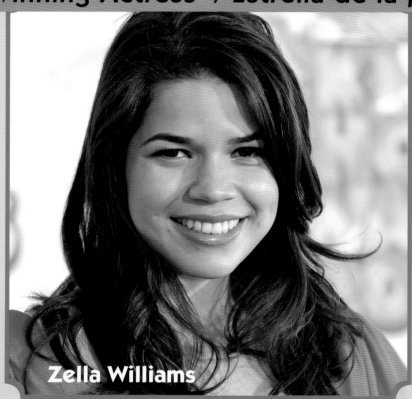

Zella Williams

PowerKiDS press ™ & **Editorial Buenas Letras**™
New York

Published in 2011 by The Rosen Publishing Group, Inc.
29 East 21st Street, New York, NY 10010

First Edition

Editor: Joanne Randolph
Book Design: Kate Laczynski
Photo Researcher: Jessica Gerweck
Spanish Translation: Eduardo Alamán

Photo Credits: Cover, p. 1 Jon Kopaloff/Getty Images; pp. 4–5, 9, 18–19 George Pimentel/Getty Images; p. 6 Bruce Glikas/Getty Images; p. 7 Avik Gilboa/WireImage/Getty Images; p. 8 David McNew/ Getty Images; p. 10 Randall Michelson/Getty Images; p. 11 Frederick M. Brown/Getty Images; p. 12 Jeff Kravitz/FilmMagic/Getty Images; p. 13 (top) Maury Phillips/WireImage/Getty Images; p. 13 (bottom) Fred Hayes/WireImage/Getty Images; pp. 14–15 Matthew Simmons/Getty Images; p. 16 George Napolitano/FilmMagic/Getty Images; p. 17 Jemal Countess/Getty Images; p. 20 Steve Granitz/ WireImage/Getty Images; p. 21 Frazer Harrison/Getty Images Entertainment/Getty Images; p. 22 Jesse Grant/Getty Images.

Library of Congress Cataloging-in-Publication Data
Williams, Zella.
  America Ferrera : award-winning actress = estrella de la pantalla / Zella Williams. — 1st ed.
      p. cm. — (Hispanic headliners = Hispanos en las noticias)
  Includes bibliographical references and index.
  ISBN 978-1-4488-4895-9 (paperback Selena Gomez/America Ferrera)
  1. Ferrera, America, 1984—Juvenile literature. 2. Actors—United States—Biography—Juvenile literature.
3. Hispanic American actors—Biography—Juvenile literature. I. Title.
  PN2287.F423W5518 2011
  791.4302'8092–dc22
  [B]
                                                    2010010300

Manufactured in China

CPSIA Compliance Information: Batch #WS10PK: For Further Information contact Rosen Publishing, New York, New York at 1-800-237-9932

CONTENTS

CONTENIDO

You may know America Ferrera as the **character** Betty Suarez in the TV show *Ugly Betty*. She also played Carmen in a well-liked movie called *The Sisterhood of the Traveling Pants*. Ferrera worked hard to become an actress and to get these parts. Judging from the awards she has won, her hard work was worth it!

Ferrera is shown here at the first showing of *The Dry Land*. She had a lead part in this movie.

Aquí vemos a Ferrera en el estreno de la película *The Dry Land*, en la que participó como actriz.

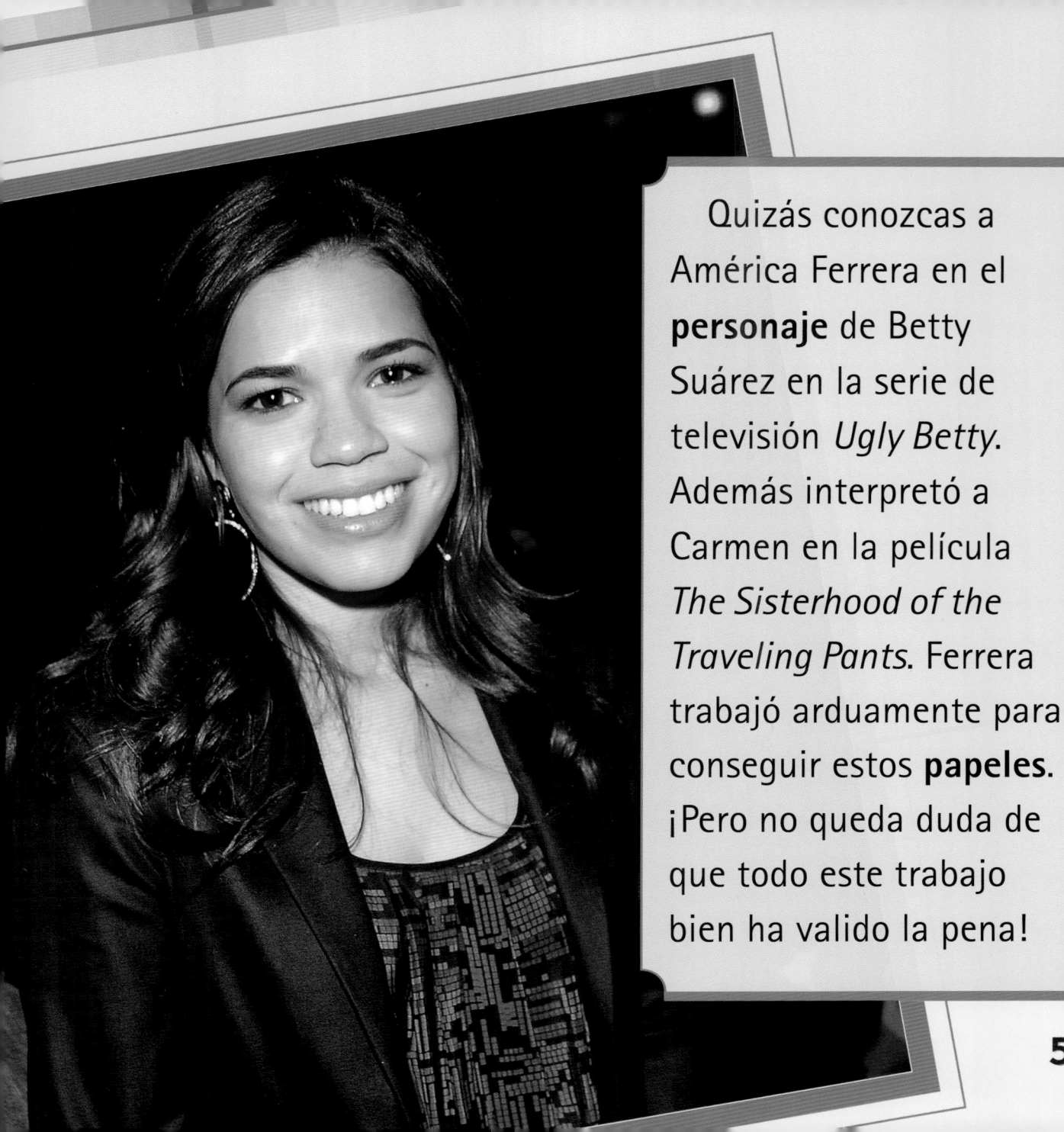

Quizás conozcas a
América Ferrera en el
personaje de Betty
Suárez en la serie de
televisión *Ugly Betty*.
Además interpretó a
Carmen en la película
*The Sisterhood of the
Traveling Pants*. Ferrera
trabajó arduamente para
conseguir estos **papeles**.
¡Pero no queda duda de
que todo este trabajo
bien ha valido la pena!

America Georgina Ferrera was born on April 18, 1984. Named after her mother, she was the sixth child born to her parents. America's parents had moved to Los Angeles, California, from Honduras before they had their first child. Her mother **divorced** America's father after America was born.

Here Ferrera spends some time with her mother and one of her sisters.

Aquí vemos a Ferrera con su madre y una de sus hermanas.

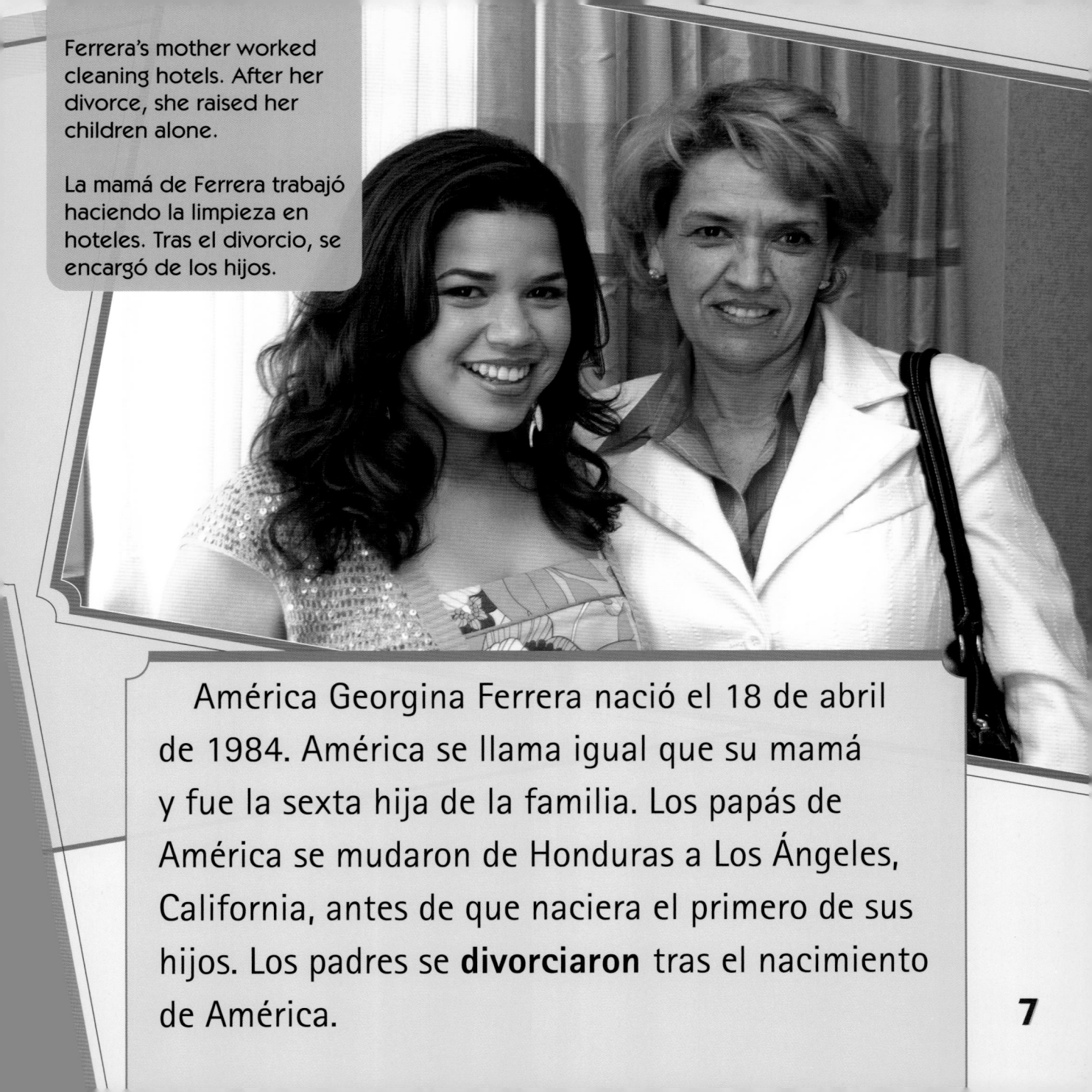

Ferrera's mother worked cleaning hotels. After her divorce, she raised her children alone.

La mamá de Ferrera trabajó haciendo la limpieza en hoteles. Tras el divorcio, se encargó de los hijos.

América Georgina Ferrera nació el 18 de abril de 1984. América se llama igual que su mamá y fue la sexta hija de la familia. Los papás de América se mudaron de Honduras a Los Ángeles, California, antes de que naciera el primero de sus hijos. Los padres se **divorciaron** tras el nacimiento de América.

7

America Ferrera's mother raised her children in Woodland Hills, a Los Angeles neighborhood. She made sure they understood how important school was. Her hard work paid off. America was **valedictorian** of her high-school class. All six Ferrera children went to college, too. America **attended** the University of Southern California.

Ferrera went to the University of Southern California, shown here, in Los Angeles.

Aquí vemos la Universidad del Sur de California, en Los Ángeles, a la que asistió América Ferrera.

Ferrera worked hard in her studies. She works just as hard in her job as an actress.

Ferrera estudió tan arduamente como lo ha hecho en su trabajo como actriz.

La mamá de América crió a sus hijos en el barrio de Woodland Hills, en Los Ángeles. La mamá de América sabía lo importante que son los estudios, y el esfuerzo tuvo sus recompensas. América culminó la secundaria en el cuadro de honor. Los seís hermanos Ferrera asistieron a la universidad. América **asistió** a la Universidad del Sur de California.

America Ferrera knew from an early age that she was interested in acting. She played a small part in *Hamlet* at her school when she was 7. At age 10, she played the Artful Dodger in *Oliver!* Ferrera landed her first movie **role** at age 16. She played a cheerleader in the movie *Gotta Kick It Up*!

Ferrera paid for her own acting classes and rode the bus to try out for parts.

Ferrera pagó de su bolsillo sus clases de actuación y tomó el autobús para ir a las pruebas.

Ferrera is shown here speaking to students at Venice High School in 2002.

Aquí Ferrera le habla a los estudiantes de la secundaria Venice en 2002.

Desde pequeña, América sabía que quería ser actriz. Cuando tenía 7 años de edad, participó en la obra *Hamlet* en su escuela. A los 10 años, interpretó a Artful Dodger en *Oliver!* A los 16 años fue seleccionada para su primer papel en una película. América interpretó a una porrista en la cinta *Gotta Kick It Up!*

11

America Ferrera appeared in another movie in 2002. She got the lead part in *Real Women Have Curves*. Ferrera played Ana Garcia. This character was a young Hispanic woman who wanted to go to college. Instead she worked for her family's clothing factory. Ferrera won awards for her work in this movie.

Here Ferrera stands with the other actors in *Real Women Have Curves*.

Aquí vemos a Ferrera con los otros actores de *Real Women Have Curves*.

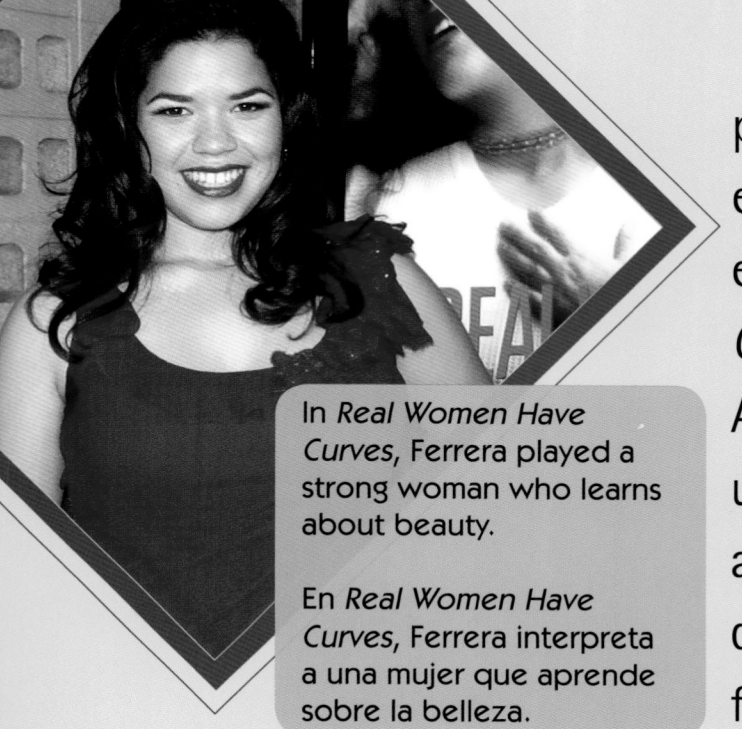

En 2002, América Ferrera participó en otra película. En esta ocasión tuvo el papel estelar en *Real Women Have Curves*. Ferrera interpretó a Ana García. El personaje era una joven hispana que quería asistir a la universidad, pero que tenía que trabajar en la fábrica de ropa de su familia.

In *Real Women Have Curves*, Ferrera played a strong woman who learns about beauty.

En *Real Women Have Curves*, Ferrera interpreta a una mujer que aprende sobre la belleza.

Ferrera is shown here with Lupe Ontiveros, who played Ana's mother in *Real Women Have Curves*.

Aquí vemos a Ferrera con Lupe Ontiveros, quien era la mamá de Ana en la película.

America Ferrera's **career** started to take off. Her next big part was as Carmen in *The Sisterhood of the Traveling Pants*. This movie came out in 2005. It is about a group of girls who stay in touch as they go off to college. A magic pair of pants helps them stay friends and work through their problems.

Ferrera starred in *The Sisterhood of the Traveling Pants* with Blake Lively, Amber Tamblyn, and Alexis Bledel.

Ferrera trabajó en *The Sisterhood of the Traveling Pants* con Blake Lively, Amber Tamblyn y Alexis Bledel.

Pronto, la **carrera** de América Ferrera se disparó. Su siguiente papel fue el de Carmen, en *The Sisterhood of the Traveling Pants*. Esta película se estrenó en 2005. Se trata de un grupo de amigas que se mantienen en contacto cuando van a la universidad. Un par de pantalones mágicos les ayuda a mantener su amistad.

Salma Hayek came to America Ferrera in 2006. Ferrera had made a name for herself as an actress. Hayek wanted Ferrera to play the lead role in a new TV series called *Ugly Betty*. This series was based on a show called *Betty La Fea*, which was well liked in Colombia. This part has earned Ferrera a lot of awards.

The Betty Suarez character works for a fashion magazine.

El personaje de Betty Suárez trabaja para una revista de moda.

Here some of the actors from *Ugly Betty* get ready to give a talk about the show.

Algunos de los actores de *Ugly Betty* se preparan para dar una entrevista.

Salma Hayek se acercó a América Ferrera en 2006. Ferrera se había ganado un nombre como actriz. Hayek quería que Ferrera interpretara el papel principal en una serie de TV llamada *Ugly Betty*. La serie se basa en un show muy famoso en Colombia llamado *Betty, la fea*. Este papel le ha dado a Ferrera muchos premios.

17

Even while working on *Ugly Betty*, America has had some movie roles, too. Some of the other movies she has done include *Muertas*, *The Sisterhood of the Traveling Pants 2*, and *The Dry Land*. She was also a voice actress in two **animated movies**. She was Fawn in *Tinker Bell* and Astrid in *How to Train Your Dragon*.

The Dry Land had the honor of being shown at the Sundance Film Festival in 2010.

The Dry Land tuvo el honor de estrenarse durante el Festival de Cine de Sundance en 2010.

América ha trabajado en algunas películas durante su trabajo en *Ugly Betty*. Algunas de las películas son: *Muertas*, *The Sisterhood of the Traveling Pants 2*, y *The Dry Land*. Además usó su voz en dos **películas de animación**. América fue Fawn en *Tinker Bell* y Astrid en *How to Train Your Dragon*.

America Ferrera has had quite a career so far!
She was the first TV actress to win three awards
in one year as a lead actress on a TV show. She won
a Golden Globe, a Screen Actors Guild Award, and an
Emmy award for her work in *Ugly Betty* in 2007. She
won many awards for *Real Women Have Curves*, too.

The cast and crew of *Ugly Betty* celebrate their Golden Globe win in 2007.

El elenco de *Ugly Betty* celebra su triunfo en los Globos de Oro en 2007.

Ferrera won an Alma Award in 2008. The Alma Awards honor Latino entertainers.

Ferrera ganó el Premio Alma en 2008. Éste es un premio para estrellas latinas.

¡América Ferrera ha tenido éxito muy rápido! Ferrera se convirtió en la primera actriz de TV en ganar tres premios como protagonista en un mismo año. Ganó un Globo de Oro, un Premio del Gremio de Actores, y un Emmy, todos por su trabajo en *Ugly Betty* en 2007. También ganó muchos premios por *Real Women Have Curves*.

21

America Ferrera has played many roles that honor her Hispanic background. She has also picked roles that show the strength of women and the beauty of difference. The list of awards America Ferrera has won is a long one. Whatever may lie ahead for her, it will be fun to watch!

América Ferrera ha interpretado muchos papeles que honran su herencia hispana. Además, Ferrera ha elegido papeles que muestran la fuerza de las mujeres y la belleza de la diversidad. La lista de premios de América Ferrera es muy larga. Habrá que estar pendientes de qué otras sorpresas nos deparará su futuro.

GLOSSARY

animated (A-nuh-mayt-ed) Gave life to. In movies, has to do with giving life to drawings or cartoons.

attended (uh-TEND-ed) Went to.

career (kuh-REER) A job.

character (KER-ik-tur) A person in a story.

divorced (dih-VORST) Ended a marriage.

role (ROHL) A part played by a person or thing.

valedictorian (va-luh-dik-TOR-ee-un) The student with the highest grades and the one who generally gives a speech at graduation.

GLOSARIO

asistir Ir a algún sitio.

carrera (la) Un trabajo.

divorcio (el) Terminar un matrimonio.

papeles (los) Las partes que interpretan los actores en una película u obra de teatro.

películas animadas (las) Películas que dan vida a caricaturas o dibujos.

personaje (el) Una persona en una historia.

INDEX

ÍNDICE

WEB SITES / PÁGINAS DE INTERNET

Due to the changing nature of Internet links, PowerKids Press and Editorial Buenas Letras have developed an online list of Web sites related to the subject of this book. This site is updated regularly. Please use this link to access the list:
www.powerkidslinks.com/hh/ferrera/